DEL BAC

poems by

Liza Porter

Finishing Line Press
Georgetown, Kentucky

DEL BAC

Copyright © 2023 by Liza Porter
ISBN 979-8-88838-297-4 First Edition
All rights reserved under International and Pan-American Copyright Conventions. No part of this book may be reproduced in any manner whatsoever without written permission from the publisher, except in the case of brief quotations embodied in critical articles and reviews.

Publisher: Leah Huete de Maines
Editor: Christen Kincaid
Cover Art: Susan Cummins Miller-Fumerole, Hverir, Iceland
Author Photo: Andrea Conway
Cover Design: Elizabeth Maines McCleavy

Order online: www.finishinglinepress.com
                also available on amazon.com

Author inquiries and mail orders:
Finishing Line Press
P. O. Box 1626
Georgetown, Kentucky 40324
U. S. A.

Table of Contents

Del Bac 1
The Major 3
Going Home 4
The Anorexic 5
Say we had poetry then 6
Adagio for Strings 8
California Poppies 10
There, doctor 11
The Wall 12
Before the Voice 13
Body Count 15
Red Stain 16
Safe Sky 20
In the Back Yard 22
Work Furlough 24
The Chained-Man's Apprentice 25
Everything He Says 26
Bobby 27
A Fetus in Winter 28
Susan. Think of all the fibers 29
Let Me Return 30
The Blue 32
In Coolidge, Arizona 33
When I call 34
Far Line 35
Twenty questions / 16 yesses 36
First meeting. 38
Sit and Listen 39

Came to believe	40
The Old Man's Legs	41
There, he says	42
Disappeared	44
Sylvia	45
Stop and Tell Me	47
Freshly Painted Walls	49
The White Piano	50
Mrs. Stevens	51
I wish I had a river	53
Edie, if you hear Dylan singing	54
Keep the singing	55
My grandmother's room, its clean linoleum floor	56
Something Good Just the Same	57
Trains	59
No	61
Her Sharp Tongue	62
The Light	63
At the stop sign	64
To Joy Harjo on the Radio from New Mexico	65

*Seeing words as angels, as independent carriers of soul …
saves us from the suffocating thought that speech is no more
than the utterance of personal opinions.*

Paul Matthews

Del Bac

1.
In Tucson, dust rises from the land
so close to her, she can cup it in her hands.
She stirs her tea, speaks softly
to describe this: what she would do if she could
make the rivers run again.

Del bac she is called. Or *punta de agua,*
the Spanish words overriding the Pima.
It is true water used to rise up
from underground and flow out
at certain points as if a fountain. So much water
it couldn't remain in the dark reaches of the earth.
Decades ago, she says.

Now she wears long sleeves, a wide-brimmed
hat made of dust to keep out the sun. Sweat is stitched
into the fabric. When I look for myself in her,
where a cool reflection used to exist, there is none.

But she and I are alike. When we look
at something, we see only that. Lack of water
does not lend itself to misinterpretation.
When we hear its flow, it is something
taking place in the past. When I talk to her
I think she will last only a few more years.

2.
Sometimes in winter, she returns to us.
It's been several years since the Tanque Verde
swam into the Pantano, twice as many
since the Santa Cruz flew back and forth
across its banks. Even her tears make
no indentation on this parched land. Her eyes flit
across the Sonora like great-horned owls
looking for a place to nest.

It is simple. She comes to embrace the rain,
to ask for our redemption. She glides over
the surface of the wash looking for signs
of wet earth, she listens to something existing
long ago. I know what she will say many years
from now. Or tomorrow.

This winter, water returned to Sabino Canyon.
They say the falls are dangerous, people
are drowning in ignorance, the mountain lion
has come to claim its home. We startle at his presence,
put up signs, say someone must do something.
She comes to see if we will learn anything at all from
too many people in the eastern bosque, too much raped land
in the north. Her mouth is dammed by those
who would take her body. She hides from
our lack of compassion.

3.
The Catalinas? A mound of sticks and bones
burned to the ground last year. There is no word
in English to describe her sorrow. *Del bac* says it all.
Her constant underground weeping, her wish
to become. She has everything we could want.
In the morning, I watch paloverde blossoms fall
to the earth like yellow tears, a sure sign of
summer's coming. I write poetry instead of dancing
for rain, it accomplishes nothing. The river bed
gives nothing. She has come to expect nothing
from us but abandonment.

Del bac has many different paths. The desert
holds them out, calls her to them. I am so thirsty,
who drinks her endlessly like the rest. She is as
far away as the clouds and thunder of monsoons.
There is no way to rush them but the waiting.
Del bac, who knows exactly how long it takes
for any river wash to reach another.
Any drop of rain.

The Major

What you have heard is true. I was at his house.
His children sat at the dinner table like soldiers.
There were newspapers, cloth napkins, cases of
bourbon in a closet with his Marine Corps dress
blues and his gun. The sun was a bruised cheek
falling into the ocean. The windows of the house
were locked. Unspoken words hung on the chain-
link fence in the back yard like escaping
convicts. Walter Cronkite recited body counts
from the living room. He named no names. We ate
roast beef, potatoes, carrots. All the children were asked
what they'd learned in school that day. When the youngest
didn't answer, the Major took a sip of his drink
and went on to the next one. "Nothing," he said, his face
a war mask. The rest of them inhaled in unison. The older girl
said to the younger with her elbow: *Say nothing*. The older boy
said in a soft voice, eyes down: "I learned something in Latin
today." The dog licked my hand under the table. No one
looked up from their food. The butter melted in its crystal dish.
The grandmother said "More biscuits?" and offered the plate
to the mother, who shook her head and stood up.
"Dessert?" she said. They all looked at her like puppies ready for
a leash and an open door. The Major said: "They eat too much
as it is," and drank more whiskey. The grandmother stood
and started to clear the dishes. The boy who had learned nothing
stood, too. The chair legs scraped the floor. The Major gulped
the rest of his drink, knuckles white around the glass. "Sit down,"
he said. The boy who had learned nothing ignored him
and kept walking. The sisters held hands under the table.
The dog's tail tickled my bare leg. The dog growled.

The form and tone of this poem were borrowed
from "The Colonel" by Carolyn Forche

Going Home

When I go back after thirty years and the old man
asks me in, the light almost blinds me, this God-white presence—
his wife, resting, a week past breast surgery—
her beatific smile, the recliner placed where
a dividing wall used to be. *They got it all*, the old man beams
and shows me outside, the back yard a jungle, the exact one
I'd dreamed of, wildflowers and blooming citrus and smooth green
grass. I remember my grandmother's sweet peas along the back fence,
lavender and pink and white, and the ghost-yellow lawn that never
quite thrived, you could have flamed the whole fucking thing with a single
smoking match.

The Anorexic

She screams Dutch:
Bastard! Her voice
guttural. I see

neck bones through pink
skin, his nod, his
prick pulse, his snake

tattoo. She won't
eat. She listens to
Sound of Music over

and again in those
drugged streets. Dreams
edelweiss

days. Her soul
escaped. Some sort
of homeland. On her

bedroom door
jamb, his Germanic
grin. She dreams

a judge's booth. A
noose. I say: It's
all where

you stand, it's
charred grass. She
screams: hanging! I say

wrong direction. She
says visions keep her
living. Her black

rage. His face
suspended in
mid-rape.

Say we had poetry then.

Something to pull our drowning bodies
out of the sea of fear we struggled in every day.
Say we sat in the dark of our room, backs against your twin bed,
feet pointed toward mine, toenails shining
under the moon as it peeked through a crack
in the drapes, a small flashlight illumining the pages
of some book that appeared from the sky—*Out of nowhere*
we would say—*maybe God sent it.*

Say we had poetry then and the words in that book
pierced our hearts as cupid would much later in our lives, opened them wide
with awe and wonder, like the hymns we'd sing in church choir
dressed in pale blue robes performing the same way we had to
the rest of the week at home. Say this book of poems
fell from the sky into our laps one night, the words
filling our souls with so much light
we couldn't hold it, we would burst into stars
we had to make up our own songs—me the melody, you the harmony,
and those songs were ours, forever, we would never forget them.

Say we had poetry then and our songs drifted out the cranked-open window
and floated into that southern California night, the sky
balmy with the ocean so close by, what if our voices
swam into the mist that gathered in droplets on car windows
by morning and burned off by noon, like the blue fog did
each Sunday on the coast in summer, by the time we got to our haven,
the ocean, and ran from the station wagon across the sand into the waves
without a sound and floated out into the salt water
as if we'd found a new womb to rock us.

Say we had poetry then, and our songs flew out the open window
of our room and into the neighbors' houses the next morning through
screen doors, the sound so sweet—who can possibly resist the voices of
innocent girls—and what if those songs somehow transformed their lives,
as they couldn't ours, for our paths were preordained, I see now, but what if
the words that escaped from our throats back when darkness

was safer than light, when silence seemed the only reasonable reply,
say those songs actually made it out from between our lips
and helped someone live a better life. Made the Vietnam war death
of Lieutenant Jordan next door easier for his widow and daughters to bear,
made the eyes of those two ugly girls in the house on the other side
shine with themselves and their fate. Say we had poetry then, later,
of course, after the light became safe, after
the silence became unbearable.

Adagio for Strings

As we do this
music, this thing.
That whisper, this bruise
Barber's strings.

So separate, but joined
we sing.
And slip like liquid
down the strings.

As we do this
pleasure to
each other so
close to the pain.

As we do this
music, cells sing.
This pleasure so
close to the sting.

Reach higher each time
we scream. Every
time we
do, we change.

As we do this
pleasure to
each other so
close to the pain.

As we do this
music, I weep.
No time
no space, the strings

so high, then
quiet again, so
soon past screaming
the pain.

As we do this
pleasure
to each other
close to the pain.

California Poppies

On a mild winter day
I walked there, to the beach

and gathered the rusted gold seaweed.
I saw a stone with markings,

stripes from shells, or symbols,
heard the wind blow its wise, wild words.

And perched on the shore
a seagull, white and gray, dying.

Later, I sat on the dunes
with their sparse grass, I slept,

dreaming of old things, and walked
on the azure sea.

It had swept people in fluorescent boats
beyond the headlands

and pushed the night's bluest stars
into the sky, and from

the deepest darkness
an ancient lighthouse lit the water.

Off on an island, my dream-self
stepped into a wideness of waves

and floated on the sea
with California poppies,

their flaming orange petals like life rafts
miles from where they belonged.

after Philip Levine

There, doctor

> *Here is the adrenaline rush you crave…*
> *that insane puncture into heat and blood*
>   from "Here, Bullet" by Brian Turner

If my spirit is what you wanted, then there,
doctor, is the virginity I owned at birth,
my legs in your cold metal stirrups, my knees

saluting the ceiling, my compulsive wish to please.
There, is the knifing of my thighs, your face hangs over
me like a god, I dare you to keep going.

Because there, oh, learned doctor, inside your cravings
is where I suck and spit the secrets you groomed me with.
And there is my open heart, that electric pulse of thought

and feeling when one is young and free or blind.
There, fine doctor, are my flesh and veins and bones
you wanted so badly to own.

I invade the core of your mouth, I slash your tongue out.
And there, supposed healer, is where I shut my eyes,
take a breath and scream.

But here, sick doctor is where I vomit your cock's orders,
here is where my skin and muscles and soul refuse to
acknowledge your tricks, yes, they're embedded in me,

each tainted act still gouges deep. But here, doctor,
calculating groomer, high class impostor, here is where
I wake, here is where my eyes open and see.

The Wall

Camp Pendleton, Winter 1967

The east end of the swimming pool is fifteen feet deep
where Sgt. Dalton orders his Marines to heave themselves
off sky-high platforms in full war-time gear, while we,
the innocents, start swim practice at the far end, Sgt. D
yelling at us from his corner. Our small forms swim, shallow to deep
as darkness comes, fifty meters up and back the black-lined
lanes of that heated pool, our limbs disappear into mist
in the shallows, the pool lights illumine us
like ghosts floating in some murky turquoise lagoon,
our mothers shiver in blankets wrapped like shrouds.
Do they ever hold their breath like the mothers of boys going off to war
hold theirs, like we in that safe pool hold ours between strokes,
do the mothers ever fear their children will disappear, they'll never
actually touch the far wall and come back, little robots with machine gun arms,
pumping hearts in training for the inevitable skirmish with the enemy
at next weekend's swim meet. Each time I swim past the point
where shallow drops abruptly to deep, where Marines not much older than me
are trying to survive that wet green vastness on the other side
of the planet, I look down at the ominous drop and wonder if I have the guts
to stop and hold my breath, to dive down and grab that underwater wall—
walk myself hand by hand down its rough concrete, all the way to
the bottom, lungs full to bursting, fingers small suckers on that painted surface.
No gear on my back, nothing but my slick young body in its red white & blue
striped suit, I keep going, staring into the chasm, and wonder if
there's some halfway point out in the Pacific, perhaps the same spot
they say the international date line is, where a wall like this,
only thousands of feet deeper, divides the earth into two distinct pieces,
I wonder if anyone has ever tried to pull herself down
to see if there's a doorway there, somewhere, and I want to know
if anyone has ever really gotten
to the bottom of anything in this world without dying.

Before the Voice

> *...to mimic an earth-toned reptile*
> *in this dusky land.*
> —Susan Cummins Miller

I could do blend in,
fake okay, wear clothes
no one notes. How to

grit teeth at animal growls
turn head to stuff
my own. I was

taught not to talk back
as fists pound. Pretend
deaf ears, honed these

skills like a craftsman does. I knew
sledge hammers and rusty nails
to hold mouths shut. Small

girl jokes, cute-ness
instead of talk. I liked
blank, plain, cleaned my plate for

mother's smile. When the
storms came, saw
nothing wrong, closed my

blue eyes. When
dogs died
cried dry tears, watched

fur and bruised bones. I could
lower my eyes, say yes, sir,
come when I was told. I didn't

rock boats, fish for truth,
recognize my own face.
I could do lizard, gecko, twisted mute,

fool, anything else you can name.

Body Count

I think I prayed back then in the dim basement of the church where the preacher cooked pancakes in the morning before school and tried to teach us the Bible, we sat in a sleepy stupor on the floor of a storage room painted black for the drama of it, the Beatles in their day-glo suits on the walls and ceiling created by meticulous boys still too young for the dirt of war, I think I prayed when Danny Jones tried to kiss me one Sunday night, the turntable spinning Simon and Garfunkel looking for America, the Greyhound bus coaxing me away—from the war, from his tongue in my mouth, I think I prayed he would understand my hesitation was not just him but the news and the fighting, my father's fists, the body counts, the body counts, the wrongness of boys like him dying each and every day and Cronkite announcing the number every night, the horror of anything having to do with me or him or our safe little playpen on the floor of the basement of a church where the preacher tried to teach us Love and Peace and Jesus, Joan Baez's high and sad voice floating out from the scratchy turntable speaker, her pure sweet voice calling to us like the Angel of Death.

Red Stain

1. (in answer to her letter)

In the north San Joaquin Valley
capitol domes and dust, she writes:
We will get a house together, white picket fence,
the two of you and the baby
you fear is forming inside you. You see
rusty-red stain on green carpet, empty
Gallo bottles, that boy's face over you, starched
white shirt, Santana so loud
your ears drum, puffs of smoke from the briquette factory
south of where you all went to school, dust
rising from fat bicycle tires, cigarette butts
next to the railroad track, half-smoked joints, a pale blue phone
that never rings.

2. (equilibrium)

Illicit drugs work, hashish chopped into tiny chunks,
hand-made pipes, make sure just enough smoke holes
are pricked in the tin-foil bowl, use a bent paperclip.
Equilibrium means not being able to see straight.
The blood doesn't come, you wake in the night
at the slightest sound, the red stain almost
dull brown now. Benzedrine pills are good,
banana daiquiris, anything with at least
a slight acidity. There is a doctor involved
in all this, his hourly rate reasonable when you don't
calculate his lecher-eyes or dope in exchange for
prescriptions and lies. He hides both in the drop-down
ceiling tiles of his office. *I shouldn't
be alone here with you,* a smirk on his clown face.
Maybe you should go on the pill, your legs up in stirrups.

3. (latter day saints)

What to do with the red stain
but cover it up with a rag rug. You don't need pregnancy
explained, or the difference between boys and girls. Or
virginity. Statutory rape might take a while. Maybe
decades. You respond to her letter and wait.
And wait. You suppose this limbo has nothing to do
with the Mormon boy who held your hand on "J" street in
the rain. They were Neighbors,
they traded Notes.
I've never felt anything like this, Joseph Smith's progeny
pronounces beside you. Even a trip north
doesn't solve it. You can't close your eyes
to everything and hope to survive. Pharmaceuticals work
as long as no one else is around. Diet pills. Or two packs of Kools
a day, three on weekends, eight-packs of Diet RC every 24 hours
in bottles you have to return, unless you want
piles of glass on the floor in the corner.
His face on your neck, red-veined eyes, nothing to see but the teeter-totter
of push-ups. Fuck. Fuck. Fuck.

4. (purple haze)

The next time you hear from her she wants to borrow
fifty dollars to become a Scientologist. No mention
of picket fences, rocking chairs, humming in the night.
The doctor hints something happened to you.
Nothing, really, you think, except his eyes shifting
as you walk into his office. But this is improper
talk. No one mentions
squinted eyes, muscled farm-boy hands
biceps straining, Levi's round your knees,
who's responsible for birth control in these situations.
The relief felt by both of you
for different reasons. *Thank God
he was young enough to stay hard*, she says,
I've heard they kill you then. This was date-rape

after all, though you don't recall being asked out
in the first place. Nor did he ask in. It takes
years to know or say this. The cop who wants
a long distance play-by-play decades later
jacking off at the other end of
the phone. The oxygen sucked out of the air. Rug burn on your ass,
shattered glass. A certain struggle, though who
could say, the needle on the record player scratching,
scratching, no Sweet Baby James this time, just
Hendrix in his purple haze. Ears plugged, amazing
without any fingers. Magic.

5. (swimming)

I was a fish in polluted water, you tell her. Like molasses.
This is what it is to lose what you never had in the first place.
*When the math teacher fucked you, did you fight back
or just give in?* There is much to be said
for acquiescence. *Did you want it?* They say
that is the true question. She scratches dry skin
on her face, flips her brittle hair around cheek bones
as visible as prison fences, there is nothing in her stomach
for more than a few long minutes at a time. Is this
when you start spending hours again on your knees
in front of the toilet bowl? Or chewing and spitting in the garbage
can? Whole pages of yearbook scribbles reflected in white porcelain. You can
clean it for days at a time, no Playtex gloves,
Comet-shredded hands only remind you of the boy
from the sticks who couldn't wait to close the door behind him
on the way out, his aftershave swimming with come.
There is never enough Clorox.

6. (reunion)

I dated this old guy, she says, *a cop, balls
down to his knees*. Laughing. *I could never say no.*
She still weighs 92 pounds. You still vomit almost everything
that goes into your mouth. You never say the word.

_____.

No one does. Secrets pound you like rubber stamps
on junk mail. The back of your hair in snarls
like a baby left too long sleeping in a crib. There is
no baby. Definitely no picket fence. Your mouth
good for only two things. In and out. In and out.
What does this make you think of? says the bleach-blonde girl
in platform shoes in a movie thirty years later, riding an exercise bike
skin-tight pink spandex at the gym. *Did you deduct
15 pounds for your shoes?* the other girl asks
at the scales. The dark theater shakes with laughter. You can't see that
chick-flick enough times. Once even twice in a row. You either
hate it or love it. The dance scene makes you
weep every time. *Time after time.* Baby blue and pink
shimmering satin, *such style, such cute accents
around the mini-dress hems*, pronounces the Vogue editor.
Neither of you show at the ten-year reunion.
Or the next.

7. (two balloons)

You can't recall his face. *At least he had the decency to
go, at least he didn't try to hand you
a twenty-dollar bill,* she says. *That happened to me one time.*
Oh, he paid you all right. Thirty years of denial
is enough lucre for a lifetime. He wore
cowboy boots. Pointed toes, weapons of lethal destruction
if he'd ever kicked or took one in his hands. You see brown
scuffed heels wore down, cowshit on the bottom
for all you know. Funny how you can be floating
on the ceiling and still lie flat on the floor.
My hands felt just like two balloons,
the British rocker croons. *I am comfortably numb.*
That's it. Exactly. Perfect.

Safe Sky

If you walk east from this desert,
you might see flowers or
clouds, the sky we always wanted
but couldn't quite grasp.

What turned us all into caricatures
of ourselves, into statues
carved from the stones
our mothers threw, hoping

they differed from the ones
they'd juggled before our time?
But maybe the sky should not be envied
with its moods, its too many

colors, its choice of moon or sun,
stillness or wind, its ability to destroy.
We have more choices than they
did, those women whose minds

weren't often allowed to bloom,
their eyes sad much of the time
longing for safe sky.
But we didn't fight that war,

the one that saved the world,
and ours did nothing of the sort,
and now all they accomplish
is repetition. As if the men

who run the world
from their glass houses,
their gallons of golden oil
dripping like time into

bottomless holes
are incapable of perceiving
that if they let us in
we would not have to

heave our stones
or chisel away at their hearts
or pick up our shovels
to bury them first.

In the Back Yard

This is a good time to listen
for the sounds of songwriters with no
instruments to play, who know what it's like
to sing through mesquite limbs, a good place
to see where winter has stripped the branches
of mulberry trees, their missing leaves
humming the songs of a brutal nation.

I sit here and hear cars suck up pieces of
broken notes into their bellies, spit out
the accepted compositions, translations,
hear the last dog bark its pitiful song of hope,
knowing not so long from now the silence will choke us
with cracked glass, the way sleet takes
all breath away and flings it to the frozen ground.

I was born with violence in my ears,
so it is easy to think bombs are falling like ice
from a cold sky, see birds drop to the earth
at the beginning of summer, or the way
paloverde blossoms float to the ground,
easy to taste the fear in my mouth
as war bugles or drums.

This is a lonely place, however beautiful
or quiet where a hawk perches on top of
a telephone pole, his cry held
silent inside blank musical staves waiting
for a conductor's baton to
point toward him and
instruct him to fly or sing.

I see the dried-out weeds, the four yellow blooms
of the bird of paradise still clutching their red hearts
though some inner beat will soon fell them
like anything else to the desert floor. I watch the pale sheet
of sky try to brighten the world, hear the sad
whistle of a train in the distance
as if a gray fog carries its notes

these five or ten miles
in a call for swift retreat. I study
its song as if the longing of souls to rise up
and leave their ancient homes.
I catch myself hoping
all will burn and dissolve into whiteness
so we can begin again.

Now, the mourning doves finally begin singing
the same song as yesterday
and the day before and tomorrow
and I know there are spirits calling me,
this symphony, this cacophony of
hoo-hoo-hoo and silence, train engines
rattling down steel tracks

laid long ago by enslaved railroad workers
who didn't want to be doing
what they were doing, but did it
anyway, calling and responding
to each other, their spontaneous songs
carrying them further
and further toward home.

after Scott King

Work Furlough

As you step down from the truck cab, dust swirls round your
ankles, late fall in the San Joaquin, citrus leaves brown with
dust, dust between your fingers, in your teeth, as you head
back to the camper door, his hand on the knob, haven't had a
woman in ten years, he said back on the penitentiary road, eyes
on the dashboard clock, fingers tapping, face a mask of
something like hope, the dust coats your eyelids now, heavy and hot,
there is nothing inside you now
but his hand pushing down your pants, a pinch of pain, tinge of red as he
pulls out, glances at his watch, pulls you down from the mattress,
the stuffing pokes through gaping rips in the cloth, its blue-striped ticking
mocks you, the dirty buttons follow you like eyes on your way back to town,
down the farm road back to the penitentiary
where there is nothing but men.

The Chained-Man's Apprentice

In the flats of Vacaville, gray razor-wired prison, I met a man. Welcome to the fuckin joint, he says, flint eyes blooming black stories wound like rope round my smoke-filled fingers. We chisel each other's granite hearts, prospectors' picks praying for gems, going just so far into rigid ground, hit boulders, find only mica chips, fool's rock, fake shaking fossil bones, our twin rage.

He shows me thick skin making, leather fingers freckled doubt, exercise yard sun, muscles pumped from millions of repetitions, epithets, derisions. His Trojan soul closed to all but conquering a world he never wanted.

I see a boy, dandelion yard, leather harness in place, cloth diaper, naked face. Chain hooked to clothesline, twilight trailer dust, cop murder, bruised body, grand theft auto. Now he growls at whoever happens by, white trash guards, dark-skinned brothers, his teeth yellow loyalty, starved coyote eyes never exposed to daylight, years in solitary boxed inside like unrequited love, chains and cement shit-holes symbols of unbroken will to survive.

He shows me seashell soul, new ways to bury ghosts, gives us old skeleton names. Bay Area fog is our sad breath, horror stories his great escape. Guns he made inside, machinist's hands greased with hate, well-invented shivs exquisite proof of journeyman status, earned rep no use at all outside.

I give him virgin skin, closed eyes, old assaults like magnets to his new moves, hard blue earth to stand on. We try to gash each other to marrow, conjure failed promises, surfaces too fuckin tough, grow nothing but more spines. Our wet eyes when I leave the only open sores we've ever shown.

Everything He Says

His hands make table lamps from driftwood
look like wild boars, fix old cars, machine
metal parts, says he hates the shop, too much
like the joint, too noisy, too much filth.

Black under his nails, has her clean them once
cut them, from then on she always does. She dreams
silver clippers turned into shivs
he made, he mentions the guy who could

suck his own cock, Houdini body, cons would
stop by his cell and stare. Prick coulda sold tickets
he says, one pack per peek, laugh busting up
and out, huge gush of bullets and stale air.

His head shakes then rage escapes through messy
hair he's never looked at once since parole. Who
needs mirrors, he says, we're just old faces, left
hand lights a match, one more non-filter as if his last

inhalation, or if they're driving somewhere, she does it.
Pulled over on the 50 to Tahoe maybe, eyes full of shit
to give The Man, she can see them slapping cuffs
on his wrists, body stiff iron cross, one more night in jail.

But that never happens. Never happens. Gravel spits
radio playing oh, black water, keep on, her hand on his
on the gearshift. Drifting, he calls it, a little pot, penis
out of his pants. Touch it, he says, grabs her hand.

Bobby

He tells stories smoking dope
no one listens any more,
people abandon kittens
at the end of the road, he
adopts them, chops wood,
stacks cords against walls
outside the trailer, he sees cats
shaking in the Oregon cold,
he calls it gladiator school
the place he comes from
though the arena is empty,
the wood stove
burns red hot one time
the damper open too long,
all that clean oxygen, he hears
the metal walls scream as
they cool down, he watches with
closed mouth, he fights
gang wars in dreams
tries to lay down weapons
when he plays with the kittens,
face soft as his worst meanness.

A Fetus in Winter

In the beginning he taught me to chop wood.
Axes and beer and steamy breath and 'better wear those
leather gloves, hon, you'll cut off your hand.' At the end
he took me practice driving with snow chains
all the way up into old growth forest, yelling in my ear
as the truck veered off the muddy road. Later we slipped
side by side down that same path past the barn
on something like garbage can lids with no handles.
I'd already left him once
just after the rabbit died and soon we'd divide

up everything—our dreams, our breath, even the death
between us. But this last day I slide down that hill
over and over, his blood and mine growing inside me,
and pray the danger will decide for me
instead of stumbling into the clinic the next week
my cervix twisting as if to give birth, dragging him there with me
as though performing some sort of ancient, sacred ritual.

Susan. Think of all the fibers
woven into a soul. Not

that old skin bag we stuff
the past in and sew shut, but

the gifts—cotton thread,
wool yarn, and cord.

Thread could spell the names
of those who helped.

Wool, the arms they offered.
Cord, the way we tie ourselves

to the fist-voices who would
break our teeth, our tongues.

Once, on the shore of Puget Sound
under brutal steel skies

a friend and I threw rocks
into the water, one at a time.

Each stone stood for someone
who had sewn our mouths closed

with lies. We hurled
those false voices into the Sound,

naming names, saying:
I do away with you. I do away.

Our words the thread-veins
that bound us to these others.

Our breath the glass knife
cutting them away.

Let Me Return

Let me return and start over
as a new-winged seed

sliding through the dawn, breathing
mist and light. Let me enter,

this time from above, and watch
water and rock and fire,

a flying being who nests in tall pines
knowing it will all be different

and hoping it will not. This time
let me go deep into old growth forest

and cry for the friends I have lost.
The dead have all returned

to their places and ancient ships
sail out of the harbor, their engines

break the calm into circles of dark glass.
This time I will dive into my body

and ask no questions
after wandering for centuries

one being of billions who has floated
down from the clouds and over

the hills to the sea that will never die,
a winged seed who has come home

to the light, baked and molded,
a tiny being who will unfold again

and know there is only this
one more chance to love.

after Philip Levine

The Blue

Up on the starting block loose-limbed: hope, a cloud behind
your blue eyes   the pool blue the sky blue everything so blue you
think you'll dissolve into it   the water
into the sky, the endless empty blue of a California
July   endless days on the starting block, waiting for
the gun, the bullet to pierce your ears, that slight splash
you'll hear   hitting the water, a shallow flat dive
Sgt. D. commands for two hours every afternoon, four on
Saturday   the pool the blue the bubbles rising, what
will you see as you fly off the block onto
blue glass, face tilted up and ready for the race, for that
first stroke   what will you see when you hit the blue water
flat glass shattering, your arms rotating
like windmills in the blue, swimsuit gold and blue, tanned limbs
cross the pool, tight nerves moving
through the water, a blurred fetus somersaulting at the far wall, the violent
                    pushing off, almost a birth, the surface
of the blue barely breaking as both
feet hit concrete   you make the turn Sgt. D. drilled you
on day after day, the blue of the sky pressing and
pressing, so cool cool blue water churning as you breathe,
the blue pool your blue eyes the blue sky one huge painting, shades
of blue brushed on   sky blue indigo
turquoise blue midnight blue   all the colors of blue in the entire
universe flash before you, standing and squinting
a hundred thousand years
on the starting block as you swallow your fear, as you wait for
the gun, that perfect pop, that invisible prop in a stranger's hand
that shocks you into bending breathing diving, the gun
that breaks up the blue sky and the water and your blue eyes
into perfect blue-white glitter each and every time.

In Coolidge, Arizona.

His name's Tommy
my sister has a crush on him
& his cowboy boots
& his 10-gallon hat. While we eat
Mexican, I joke that
beer works for hair of the dog, doesn't it
& he says yeah, but after a while
it's all just one big fucking
hangover.

When I call

the behavioral health place
& can only get an appointment
for next week, I know
I can't ever drink again
if I'm going to keep
that appointment.
I don't.
& I do.

Far Line

In twilight, on a road, we stop,
hearts beating like mad, the rabbit
in her frightened hesitation, ears cocked,
behind a wood slat fence.

She hears something I am deaf to.
I notice the dusk, the telephone
wire, its buzz, the way the sun
burns hotter as it slides past the far line.

She hears everything I long for—
birds rustling leaves, singing. Maybe
secret words from the first star
in the almost dark sky.

The part of me that can see one star at a time
goes with her when she flees. The rest—
my fear, the night, my stubborn silent
envy—stays here, with me.

Twenty questions / 16 yesses

Do you lose time lose time   time   time
do you lose time from work because of
drinking?
Does drinking make your home life un-
happy? unhappy?   unhappy?
Do you drink   drink   drink   because
you are shy shy? shy with other people?
Does your drinking
affect your reputation? reputation?   reputation?
Have you ever felt guilt guilt guilt   guilt
or remorse after drinking?
Have you ever been in financial
difficulties difficulties   difficulties?
as a result of drinking?
Do you turn to lower lower lower
companions & an inferior inferior
inferior environment when drinking?
Does your drinking make you careless careless?
careless? of your family's welfare?
Has your ambition ambition   ambition?
decreased since drinking?
Do you crave crave   crave?
a drink at a definite time?
Do you want want   want
a drink the next morning?
Does drinking cause you to have difficulty difficulty DIFFICULTY
in sleeping? sleeping?   Sleeping?
Has your efficiency efficiency? efficiency?
decreased since drinking?
Is drinking jeopardizing? jeopardizing
         jeopardizing your job or business?
Do you drink to escape escape   escape?
from worries or trouble? TROUBLE?
Do you drink alone? alone? alone?
         alone?
Have you ever had a complete complete loss
         COMPLETE loss of memory memory   Memory?
as a result of drinking?

Has your physician ever treated treated
treated? you for drinking? drinking?   Drinking?
Do you drink to build up your self-self-
    self-confidence? confidence?   Confidence?
Have you ever been to a hospital hospital   Hospital?
or institution institution   Institution
because of drinking? drinking?
    drinking?

First meeting.

When I finally
walk into the rooms
six months after I know
I need to &
sit down, one of the grizzly old guys
says I bet I spilled more
than you ever drank, girly!
or something
equally strange.
He's so wrong.

Sit and Listen

You belong in this room full of scruffy recovering drunks, adobe shack with cracked stained glass round its door, perched like a sinking ship on the edge of town. Smoke rises from cigarettes lodged like talking sticks in each person's fingers, blue floats just below the ceiling as if disembodied spirits long for escape through the old-fashioned wood-framed windows. Everyone has a voice here, once the leader reads the preamble and says the word topic, even the deranged, the myopic, that old man sucking oxygen from a metal tank at his feet, even the sleepy guy who just today had his last drink. Let go and let God, that man says, pouring his troubles out like cheap wine, trying not to gripe about his aggravated DUIs, two in one weekend, he says, he thrives on crisis, he says, how can he find God? he finally pleads to the group, eyes lowered like headlights bouncing off black asphalt doom. He needs to give up, he says. His fingers drum the table.

 Two young punks in muscle shirts and baggy pants glance around the room and share their horror with clear eyes and oozing wounds. Where you start is not knowing, the shaved-head boy says, an open sketchbook on the bench beside him. Pray no matter what, says the red-haired one, don't give up, he says. Surrender. A guy against the back wall cackles each time a new person talks. You want to yell at him, tell him to shut the hell up. Listen, you want to say, we're trying to save lives here, but the next voice whispers miracles, his little-kid fingers shaped into crucifixes, pit bulls that didn't attack, failed catechism classes, how when he walked in that door the first day, we were all full of shit and there was no way he could sit and listen.

 Sit & listen. The room shakes, the nervous light their tiny flames, eyes dart like snakes' tongues caught in their own lies. The next speaker smiles, lights a smoke and offers her name.

Came to believe.

There in the center of the goodwill
table is the book I read
secretly in junior high
at the town library the same year
I started drinking & using. Same:
dust jacket. Same: blue & yellow.
Same: 12 steps & 12 traditions.

The Old Man's Legs

When you come too soon to take me out of this place, I go.
Anything's better than staring at that old man's legs, all yellow
and puss-filled up from cirrhosis. Sure I'm a drunk, too, but I never
in my twenty-five years seen nothing like this, his ankles swollen fat
as healthy men's thighs, scaly & rude, his Buddha belly huge
as my 8-month pregnancy, face blank, he can't even
fuckin raise up out of that motor chair to get his bowl of mush
every day. What is he doing in this state-funded treatment place, anyway?
Staring closer at hell than anyone I've ever seen, even at the Vet's Club in Eugene,
even outside on the filthy street, even that wet brain guy down at the AA
house at the crossroads. A lost cause, I'm thinking, & this after Eva
the ex-junkie counselor who still gets drunk on weekends, lectures in group
looking right at me—there are no lost causes, baby, and by the way
you don't have a problem you are a problem—and that's when
I fade into you & your brown skin & your clean white shirt, into the dark dirt
parking lot outside the main house, cigarette smoke whispering behind
us as if the very spirit of Jesus has come to sweep me & you
& all the rest of us evil sinners away.

There, he says

There, one summer evening
a man asks me: are you
ready? his black hair, every
strand in place, tree leaves

in the still wind, he says:
to be with a man? his
warrior cheek bones, his
ancient Ford truck, his stories

of skid row, his jailed life
saved by men just like
him, the alleys don't miss
him, the hot blood of

Mad Dog and steaming piss
never call his name no
more, only the road—
There, one summer evening

he says this rock music is
from the devil, his blue cloth
rule book, his dark cliché eyes
his past crossing mine

like wild-fire, his
Baptist preacher-like way
of saving men just like
him, he says: we

are nothing and
always will be, his
laugh as high as babies'
cries, his stories of

short-order cooking, boozing
his way through
the West, his pressed
Levis, polished boots, his

vacant stare
when I talk back,
one time he says: is that
baby really mine?

Disappeared

I still count deaths I've known, watch the longest nights of our lives
shatter into wine-red slivers, ticking seconds of hope when no one but us
could stay clean. Those parched-earth days. All the unseen dangers,

secret enemies living only in our minds, nameless fears hanging
from a single light bulb above the meeting room table. I think of
general delivery. Or that place atheists go when they're lost,

our tree trunk backs as broken as any of the martyrs', the old ones'
eyes darting under 10-gallon hats, Mad Joe comatose in the corner.
I still feel the thirst of those who vanished so we would not.

We could never gather enough of our rusty weapons to protect us
from those altitudes, from the God we never knew except in the bottles
we finally smashed on the desert floor, wet eyes watching shards

scatter high as the iced moon. Everyone was a witness then. Who
could stop their palsied hands, who could possible be still with all
that silent keening, hot grief steaming over Goodwill tables

in the little house where three roads met. Jails, insanity, death,
they said. We turned to each other then. But your leaving still looms
in people's eyes, Dan, that longing huge as our ruined lives,

and we waited like saints to be cut into perfect gems by the world
we finally entered. Willingly, some would say. Right where you are,
the old ones chant night after night over the hallowed book, their faces

shadows of ancient battles and stale air. Their yellow-tipped fingers
grip mine for the closing prayer, as if it were still our last chance.

Sylvia

1.
Woman scorned.
Stringy-haired prolific.
Sister to Anne, Virginia.
Head full of hissing, drowning kittens.
Lover of gas ovens, mother to none.
Flap of thumb cut clear off
One winter's night. Snow outside.
Your feverish eyes glazed as if wiped glass
At dripping blood, at fixing
Supper for your two loves. But not you
Who are above chewing or sleep. Ascetic
Manic, Spartan gorilla, flagellator
Of self, everyone else. Your death
Weapons are meticulously chiseled
From metaphors, similes
The gods' and witches' stolen musings
Your disembodied hand snatches as if
Such candy could keep you living.

2.
We too wildly invent new selves.
Become Phaedra, Medusa, Ted Hughes.
Hear moons in cracked mirrors,
Screaming pink mouths.
Stitch velveteen in the dark. Scramble
For paper. Scribble, scribble.
My kingdom for a clean table!
We command fat-handed clocks to stop.
Hear vultures shriek at night. Their bloody
Beaks dash us to the earth.
We channel death dirges. Crave arsenic,
A bit of sleep.
We do not applaud your final solution.
Last act of creation.
Triumphant blinded flight. Gallop
Into frigid sky.
As if a greater feat than

Any Muse.
Poem. Life.

Who are you to gather last songs
Into baskets, throw apples at slimy snails.
Use Shakespeare's son as your knife,
His words the color of blood reflected
In your eyes. Rice paper torn
Into chits of who owes who. Only you
do this. Only you.

Stop and Tell Me

If you were to stop and tell me
what I could be again—

a woman who loves everything
and sings old songs only for the singing,

I might say, in this minor scale
I've practiced for years,

that it seems such a short time
since I could clear my heart and sing

of the dreams of dancing and life
and those lines wavering

just beyond sight. I would not
stand still while I sang, but ride

the notes as if great black ravens
strong enough to carry me

and my sorrow-songs on their
expansive wings. The land below

would be mist rising and fertile,
my hair waves of words,

a flag half-mast in honor to
what came before. I've sat

in too many cars racing too many
white lines into the future, thinking:

Ahead may be the perfect life,
a perfect home, some

mythical promised land where there exists
no hate, no guns, no greed.

Yes, I was that naïve. Now I know
that under all the blacktop roads

The old oil, the never-ending roar,
are children's faces pressed against the glass.

Freshly Painted Walls

                About our father who came into our room
and opened you, a baby deer sliced right down its center,
ragged wounds left to later bleed and rot, who stepped into the dark
khaki pants zipper clutched in his hands convinced by his mere gender
he had rights to anything he wanted. I conjured
cartoons—Bambi or Minnie Mouse—my back to that
thick glass screen, sound fading as I drifted into the silence
I always managed to turn on and off at will.

                Gulls crying on Del Mar beach, where marine officers
took families on Sunday and drank beer in paper cups on the concrete slab
up by the snack bar, their children floating on rubber rafts
out to sea as far as they could.   I was finally alone in the room
then, where I dreamed of Cinderella and Sleeping Beauty and
where during the day I drew hideous monsters with dark Crayola colors—
black, forest green, brown—on the freshly painted walls.

The White Piano

Someone had painted the piano white, old upright with bold tone, she would practice every day in the basement that had flooded just after the family moved in, pipes behind the new block walls burst with angry words, maybe, a sort of music for house warming. She practices in the basement and the father comes and goes, stinking of the whiskey he hides in the master bedroom closet with his military-issue gun and old footlockers packed with tarnished medals and dull black boots. She practices in the basement next to the garage full of girl scout cookies and on the opposite wall a huge Amana freezer, its key hidden upstairs so the commissary food will last all month. She practices in the basement and somewhere a voice calls "Perfect!" but not in the motel-sized house dug into the side of a hill like a bunker, she practices in the basement while her grandmother tends sweet peas and peppers against the back chain-link fence, rib roast cooking in the stainless-steel pan with potatoes and carrots. She practices in the basement while one brother shuts his bedroom door and counts pencil stubs, the other steals China figurines from glass-faced cabinets as if the whole world belongs to him. She practices the piano in the basement, the Linoleum under the damper and sustain pedals a clear lake below her feet she can barely reach, her John Thompson method books red and white in front of her, small hands struggling learn to translate the black and white notes on the page to the keys, she will find just the right tone, she will find the one that will make everyone sing.

Mrs. Stevens

She saved me, malcontent fraidycat
raised on yes, sirs, and bootstraps

mind quick as steel trap,
young hyenas yapping in my head.

Diagram this sentence, she said,
plum-plump woman with opaque stockings

road-map ankles in navy pumps,
bleached hair, make-up-caked

wrinkles as much a comfort to me
as any old hiding tree

just before all-ee-all-ee-in-come-free
someone's hands cupped at their mouth in

the southern California dusk.
Diagram this sentence, she said,

make-work a gentle gag in my mouth
to spare the other 5th-grade girls

from my babbling, some of us
with breasts, some not, our nicknames

for each other no worse than
what we called our secret selves.

Diagram this sentence, she said,
her kind voice a bell-chime

the one sustained note
that upside-down brass tulip

as welcome as sundown sleep.
as the school bell ringing

8:30 in the morning,
the clean linoleum floor

her clear eyes that read my mind
saw my sorrow-eyes, my dark nights.

Diagram these sentences, she said,
Mrs. Stevens, my meditation, Mrs. Stevens,

Zen messenger from heaven,
Diana from beyond the sky

sliding down a rainbow
when I was ten, long skirt waving,

painted fingers beckoning me
to a benevolent world, to the cover

of a quiet school room
where no one demanded I speak
when spoken to or otherwise.

I wish I had a river

can't you hear Joni's voice rain pounding on the roof early winter in Eugene isn't it the sad things that make us whole sitting on our knees in front of the stereo speakers three feet high no foundation under the tiny house and Zoe drying her lustrous long hair in front of the heater blasting hot air and dust all through the living room but missing the bedrooms especially mine where Myron the ex-football player pinned me on my foam mattress on the floor one of my last possessions, the guy said he could see music in rainbow waves hear bright colors on the playing field listen to people's best and worst thoughts I just thought he was a rude prick right after we did it he called a friend in Colorado to brag about it me me me within earshot, when I moved the foam mattress to my next little hole in the wall the bottom side's all covered in mildew, Christmas time jingle bells playing in the background everywhere I go to I can't shake the cold, the cold that year I just can't shake it.

Edie, if you hear Dylan singing

It's all right ma, I'm only crying
remember—
Mesa Ampitheater the summer Ariel
was born, my breasts leaking
milk, a scarf tied round your head
white silk trailing behind you, and then—
his harmonica wailing
into the hot steaming sky.

Keep the singing

She gave me thunder, the road
she gave me the poets, the poems,
the words still blare from the parchment
like trumpets, the ancient paper still flutters in the sun, the fog, the rain
she gave me the lips of death, Sexton, Woolf, Plath, she gave me the headlights,
a highway to follow named 61, its white line still there in the distance
like hope, my heart pulled by a long Pythagorean string down roads
filled with cars and girls and slamming screens, she pulled
the sadness from my ears and made me hear, she gave me
death and needles, neck shivers, she gave me poems
as if they were her very own, she said borrow, don't steal, she gave me
alphabets, chords, the minor keys, she gave me rock-
n-roll, she gave me the great song traveler, he still
screams from the vinyl and the tapes, she gave me something
to wait for, she gave me fate, her taste
for the way an image can slap you in the face, she gave me
longing, she gave me waiting, the desire to
keep the waiting, *keep the waiting*, she said, *not from
my lips but from theirs,* the others, the thunder, the road
the idiot wind, from the ones who sing with hidden tongues,
she gave me want and need and the ability to see,
to believe, she said don't fake it, wait for the real thing
don't fake it, don't give in she said *keep the singing*
she said *keep the singing keep the singing* she said.

My grandmother's room, its clean linoleum floor

with specks of gold, dress patterns, bolts of fabric,
thread, her dentures on the table next to the bed.

I sit on the floor and sort buttons
of all shapes and sizes—metal, cloth-covered, mother

of pearl—in the round wooden box fruitcake came in
one Christmas long before I was born.

Its pie-shaped dividers perfect to separate order from
chaos, safety from danger, myself from

everyone else. I watch her clean the Singer,
her calm hands, the small brush whisking dust away,

the miniature screwdriver opening parts so they could
be cleaned, the can of oil with its pointed tip

and strange gulping noise. I see her
unwavering touch, the way she measures and cuts

pieces of cloth on the varnished plywood board laid
across the length of her studio bed. I watch her

sew those dress pieces together, so careful, so quiet,
as if she somehow means to organize the world for me.

Something Good Just the Same

I have to go back where bear cubs danced under trees,
their mother hovering just out of sight,
stare up at the tops of pines until my eyes
are also blue sky, don't we all long for something?
and it might be too late.

                          I need to drive up
the rutted road from town and arrive on a winter's night
in '76, and watch for ice, wondering why
people live in cities when there's still something like this.
When I slide up the road to the guitar chords of Springsteen
or Neil Young, think why no one sings with the radio
any more, and how I got out of here in one piece without you.

                          I have to walk up
the old logging road running past the barn
to the top when there's been no rain for three months,
pine needles on the forest floor so dry we can't smoke
says the old man down the hill whose name
is gone, who will disappear the next year
into nothing.

                          I have to chop
the wood we got from slag piles, the chainsaw buzz
a thousand bees swarming, I feel them
sting even as the axe swings onto a piece
of the cord you stacked beside the trailer porch,
your work gloves too big for my hands,
but something good just the same.

                          I need to sit
with you inside the trailer by the stove but this time
not as a girl, and look up the hill where I played flute
in the basement of your uncle's gray block house
as our clothes dried, and watched clouds float over
the homestead, your mother cooking the foods
of your childhood.
                          I need to read

between your words to see exactly how your eyes burn,
breath hitches, hands shake just the slightest bit
while lighting a cigarette, how no one but me would notice or care.

                                        I have to swim out
from the Dorena Lake shore, naked, heart frozen,
prove I need nothing, as those women who came West
a hundred years ago could withstand anything, anything
at all, even watching myself drive east down the hill
road one last time, only once glancing back.

Trains

for E.D.

This early in the morning the clouds have cleared
and I can hear the whistle of train after train
rolling across the desert five miles south in the dark.

I remember trains, the one that carried you north
to the forest in autumn when no other mode of travel
was good enough. But we had our own, didn't we,

the warm tongue of dope, cool teeth of booze
the dirty fingers of men whose names we
never remembered no matter how hard we tried.

What was it about us we hated so much?
Sleeping in strangers' beds was easier than even
approaching that age-old question. The ratty motor lodge

just south of Newport that summer, its depression-ware
dishes in dull primary colors, the muddy spring
trickling down to the beach like blood from a cut.

No one could ever sweep all the grit off those
chipped linoleum tiles. The two brothers who owned the place,
how did the older one's hands feel on your skin?

I met a man just after you left, when we backed away
from the bar and headed out to his house
he was the nicest guy I'd ever known in my life.

But there were Nam-ghosts in those walls, shadows
of his petrified wife and kids, he had to shower
just after we did it on the living room floor.

He spread out a blanket first and quoted Genesis to me.
The tracks were just behind his back fence and I saw myself
running beside those shrieking metal rails

nothing but the clothes on my back and a photo
of you in my pocket, your scared eyes staring
at nothing. I jumped up into an empty car heading

east or west, it didn't make any difference.
When I caught my breath, I glanced back toward town.
Not a single soul was watching.

NO

> *Not knowing if the nothing existed*
> from "Sex Blood," by Margo Tamez

At daybreak, ink clouds in pink lines horizontal to the east. i'm not ready **Brute** i'm not ready or wet you don't know a thing about this, do you huge **Brute** grown man with little boy's heart, no excuses now, dark blue sky between no excuses now, **i'm** not ready *Brute* prick pushing pulsing inside me and inside i scream, eucalyptus tree slicing the morning sky *Brute,* inside **i** scream ***Brute*** but no one hears a silent scream, except those who know the brutal fuck ***Brute,*** eucalyptus tree trunk strong like girls' legs no more excuses now, fuck the fucks who taught you this **brute**? Trunk strong like girls' legs. *excuse:* prison walls; *excuse:* steel-barred cell; *excuse*: bare-butt boys, eucalyptus tree tall and grand trunk like girls' legs **brute** *excuse:* no power no love no hope; *excuse:* you don't care do you? *Brute*

No excuses! *I* was never there, so there! *brute I* am not there anymore, I was not there, **ever,** *I* am eucalyptus tree tall and grand trunk like women's legs *I* am not scared *I* am not there, you are not there, you brute, my eyes closed

I am not there no more excuses *brute* you don't sweat on me *brute* you do not crush me anymore, *brute*, strong like women's legs *I* am not scared you don't fuck me anymore you are not there any more huge brute you do not fuck Me any more ~~brute~~, tree strong like women's legs

I am not a bare-butt boy ~~brute~~ I am not a prison wall ~~brute~~ I am not a steel cage ~~brute~~

eucalyptus tree tall and grand strong like women's legs *I* am not there eyes closed *I* scream out loud now brute, strong women's legs as we do battle *I* push you out *I* yell brute *I* scream brute *I* push you out *I* naked girl naked woman scream brute strong women's legs as we do battle with the past *I* scream *I* push you off brute *I* scream out loud now brute, like this: **No. No. No. No. No.**

Her Sharp Tongue

She has to write those things.
If she doesn't
they will stay
festering sores
purple eggplant oozing
yellow liquid
only she can name.
And she will have to use
a cleaver
to cut them out.

The Light

1.
It was the light that birthed us first, slower than sunrise,
shocking us all into silence. Then the moon,
its dull plodding, reflecting our longing till morning.
When the sun appeared, some fell to their knees
and wept, others slept in timid exhaustion.
Through the light, I saw your stardust bed, body still
in the shine before us. You gave us what we thought
we had lost: children growing in the sun, love
of the blinding light, a kind of singing.

2.
We don't know this desert or anything about how
God works or any sort of plan. We think we can track
our path through time. But when the sun moves
through the sky the way a virus invades a body
or a drug tames a vein, we wonder what it's really like up there
in the clouds, that yellow star burning, one among trillions,
not strange at all to someone viewing it like you
from above. And when the moon appears before dark,
we say: we don't need you yet, our eyes are accustomed
to squinting, we wait for the black rain to heal the stinging.
Our tears mean nothing except relief from missing you.
You have no halo, no special light, but the memory of a face
as bright as that moon when darkness falls.

3.
I have light too, but not the whole thing. Of course I think:
was there something else I could have done? Do I have a monopoly
on going forward, or even round and round in my
tortured orbit? Is your light one of those stars by now?
I will some day glance sideways in the deep black and see
the brilliance of your flame. I know it will never
burn out. You are no more mine than the sky.
I will always track the light.

At the stop sign
a man, a young man, everyone's young these days
walks down the south side of Glenn, arms waving
conducting his secret song, that's all that happens, he
turns the corner, red shirt flapping, high-water pants
showing white ankles, legs moving to an inner heat
the sun beats down, his head, his red corkscrew curls
his eyes meet mine, nothing else, nothing else happens
I think: if I wasn't in this car, if my windows weren't
rolled up, he would say something, I know he wants to
sing out loud, I know inside he's singing, I wish
I knew his name, I wish I could hear his song.
      At a stop sign the other day, I have my windows down
I hear a bird singing, that's all that happens, that small
thing, me with my half-deaf ears over the hum of the engine
I hear a bird sing, I'm paying attention, the car idling
at a stop sign, the bird sings in a tree, I'm actually
paying attention, no radio playing, no thoughts rattling gray
gravel in my head, I hear a bird, that's all, a bird
I can't even name.
      At a stop sign years ago windows rolled up in the rain
I hear music, that's all that happens, I hear Barber's
Adagio for Strings, I hear those high-pitched screams
at the end, that's all, the radio station comes through
loud and clear, in the rain, in the car, I stop thinking
I pay attention, that's what happens, that's all.
I hear for once, I think I hear angels, I can't be sure
I hear singing, nothing else happens, and for a minute
or so at the stop sign, I think I hear something, I stop
thinking, I stop thinking, I stop thinking of my next drink.

To Joy Harjo on the Radio from New Mexico

The moment I first loved poetry
I heard your voice as if from a great distance—
a raven flapping its wide black wings far above the desert
and speaking in tongues. The road curved north

then straight, my thirst so large, the night so dark,
your words guiding me west along the dry river bed
snaking through town that craves the monsoon rain
to fill its throat.

I found you in the ripples of pages on a bookstore shelf,
submerged my parched heart in your poems and drank
as if a horse who'd galloped a thousand miles
to save its rider from danger.

ACKNOWLEDGMENTS

A Fetus in Winter, *Slipstream 23*, 2003
Adagio for Strings, *Diner*, 2006
At the stop sign, *Barrow Street*, 2006; *Passages North*, 2014
Body Count, *Ginkgo Tree Review*, 2006
Del Bac, *Skidrow Penthouse*, Spring 2006
Disappeared, *The Pedestal Magazine*, 2005; *Passages North* 2014
Everything He Says, *Permafrost*, 2005
Far Line, *The 2River Review*, Fall 2012
Say We Had Poetry Then, *Blue Mountain Arts*, 2006
Sit & Listen, *Passages North*, 2014
To Joy Harjo on the Radio in New Mexico, *The Red Wheelbarrow Review*, 2020
The Anorexic, *Diner*, 2006
The Chained-Man's Apprentice, *Slipstream 25*, 2005
The Major, *The MacGuffin*, Fall 2012
The Wall, *Whistling Shade*,
Trains, *Pebble Lake Review*, Winter 2005
    Poets on Prozac: Mental Illness, Treatment and the Creative Process (Johns-Hopkins University Press) 2008

No, Sit & Listen, The Old Man's Legs, The Chained-Man's Apprentice, The Anorexic, Everything He Says, Adagio for Strings, A Fetus in Winter, Bobby, Trains, Red Stain, The Major, Disappeared, and At the stop sign, appear in Red Stain, published by Finishing Line Press, 2014.

Say We Had Poetry Then, Going Home, Adagio for Strings, Keep the singing, The Major, Edie, if you hear Dylan singing, and Trains also appear in *Keep the Singing*, 2021

Liza Porter's poetry chapbook *Keep the Singing* was published by Finishing Line Press in 2021. Her poetry chapbook *Red Stain* was published by Finishing Line Press in 2014 and was finalist for both the 2015 Arizona New Mexico Book Award and the 2015 WILLA Award (Women Writing the West). Porter received the Mary Ann Campau Memorial Poetry Fellowship from the University of Arizona Poetry Center and is founding director of the Other Voices Women's Reading Series at Antigone Books in Tucson, Arizona. Her nonfiction was finalist for the Cleveland State University Essay Collection competition, the Faulkner Society Faulkner-Wisdom Narrative Nonfiction Book Award, the Tucson Festival of Books Master's Workshop Competition, and the Santa Fe Writers Workshop nonfiction book award. Her essay "Reconstructing" was first runner up for the *PRISM International* 2016 Creative Nonfiction Prize and Honorable Mention for the 42nd *New Millennium* Nonfiction Prize. Her essays and poetry have been published in numerous magazines and anthologies, including *The Write Launch, PRISM International, Chautauqua, Cobalt Review, Passages North, The Progressive, AGNI, Diner, Cimarron Review, Barrow Street, Pedestal Magazine,* and in *What Wildness is this: Women Write About the Southwest* (University of Texas Press: Austin, 2007), and *Poets on Prozac: Mental Illness, Treatment and the Creative Process* (The Johns Hopkins University Press, 2008). Three of Porter's essays have been listed as Notable Essays in *Best American Essays*. www.lizaporter.com.

www.ingramcontent.com/pod-product-compliance
Lightning Source LLC
Chambersburg PA
CBHW031126160426
43192CB00008B/1126